The Norris Family of Kent England

by Lorine McGinnis Schulze

ISBN: 978-1-987938-18-0
Publisher Olive Tree Genealogy

Over the last 40 plus years I have researched and gathered a great deal of information and uncovered many documents for my mother's ancestors in England. Pondering how best to preserve my research and share the stories of these maternal ancestors, I decided to compile books on each family surname.

Because the books were written for family, I have not cited my sources nor have I written long chapters of anecdotal stories. Instead I opted to create a chronological timeline for each generation. Images for all baptismal, marriage, burial, land records and so on that were discovered for each ancestor are also included.

If siblings were found, family group sheets are included. If they were not found, only my direct ancestor is noted. At the end of the book you will find blank pages for your own notes.

Those who want to know my sources can contact me directly through my website Olive Tree Genealogy at www.OliveTreeGenealogy.com My email is found at the bottom of each page.

I hope that readers enjoy these books and the stories of the ancestors.

Lorine McGinnis Schulze

Table of Contents

Norris Ancestors in Lenham Kent 8

Edward Norris circa 1746-1829 & Catherine Earl 9

Thomas Norris 1789-1859 & Mary Spicer 11

George Norris 1811-1871 & Hannah Philpot Golding 16

Georgiana Golding 1840-1882 & Charles Fuller 22

Norris Ancestors of Elmsted and Waltham Kent 25

John Norris 1690-1740 & Mary Carr 26

Thomas Norris 1714-? & Sarah Boughton 28

Sarah Norris 1743-1821 & Francis Allard 29

Notes 31

Norris Ancestors in Lenham Kent

My Norris line daughtered out with the birth of Georgiana, the illegitimate daughter of the widow Hannah Golding. Georgiana was baptised in Lenham England on 12 July 1840. No father's name was recorded in the church register.

The Lenham Kent baptisms show Hannah Golding, widow - daughter Georgiana baptised 12 July 1840.

On her marriage certificate dated 17 October 1858, Georgiana gave her father's name as George Norris and that was the clue I needed to allow me to find my Norris ancestors in Lenham.

Edward Norris circa 1746-1829 & Catherine Earl

The earliest Norris ancestor I have found is my 5th great-grandfather Edward Norris born circa 1746. Although I have not been able to find his parents' names, I found his marriage to Catherine Earl in Lenham in Kent England on 7 August 1773. Witnesses at their marriage were Ann Chapman and William Brizley. Banns were published on 18 July 1773 in Lenham.

Catherine was the daughter of John Earl and Sarah Raynor. She was baptised 17 September 1754 in Charing, Kent.

Edward was a pauper by 1789 according to the baptism record of his son Thomas, and in 1791 his cottage and garden in Lenham Heath was auctioned off.

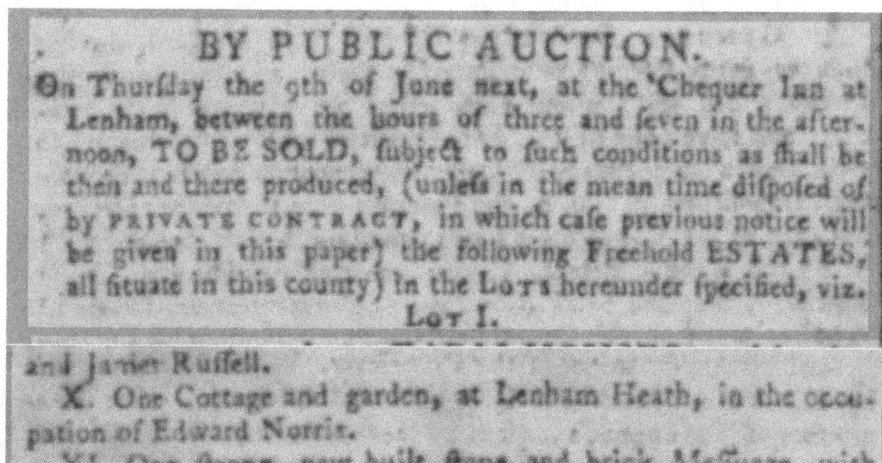

> BY PUBLIC AUCTION.
> On Thursday the 9th of June next, at the Chequer Inn at Lenham, between the hours of three and seven in the afternoon, TO BE SOLD, subject to such conditions as shall be then and there produced, (unless in the mean time disposed of by PRIVATE CONTRACT, in which case previous notice will be given in this paper) the following Freehold ESTATES, all situate in this county) In the LOTS hereunder specified, viz.
> LOT I.
>
> and James Russell.
> X. One Cottage and garden, at Lenham Heath, in the occupation of Edward Norris.

Figure 1: Kentish Gazette - Tuesday 31 May 1791

Figure 2: Burial grounds for Edward & Catherine Norris

Catherine was buried 24 December 1828 and Edward Norris was buried in Lenham on 2 May 1829, age 83. Both are buried in St. Mary's Churchyard in Lenham.

Edward and Catherine had 10 children. The list is below.

Children:	Sex	Birth	Death
Edward Norris	M	20 May 1773 Lenham, Kent England	
Thomas Norris	M	08 May 1774 Lenham, Kent England	13 May 1774 Lenham, Kent England
James Norris	M	27 Mar 1778 Lenham, Kent England	12 Apr 1840 Lenham, Kent England
Mary Norris	F	02 May 1780 Lenham, Kent England	
John Norris	M	01 Jun 1783 Lenham, Kent England	
Edward Norris	M	27 Mar 1785 Lenham, Kent England	
Sarah Norris	F	27 Mar 1785 Lenham, Kent England	
Ann Norris	F	28 Oct 1787 Lenham, Kent England	

Children:	Sex	Birth	Death
Thomas Norris	M	10 May 1789 Lenham, Kent England	28 Jan 1859 Lenham, Kent England
William Norris	M	08 Jul 1791 Lenham, Kent England	
William Norris	M	08 Jul 1792 Lenham, Kent England	
John Norris	M	04 May 1794 Lenham, Kent England	
Elizabeth Norris	F	25 Mar 1796 Lenham, Kent	04 Feb 1812 Lenham, Kent England

Thomas Norris 1789-1859 & Mary Spicer

My 4th great-grandfather Thomas Norris was baptised in Lenham on10 May 1789 to Edward and Catherine Norris. The family was noted as being paupers. A workhouse existed in Lenham, Hollingbourne District from 1730 on.

He may be the Thomas Norris who married Mary Spicer in All Saints Church in Maidstone in 1809. We know his wife's name was Mary but no surname has been found in baptisms of their 10 children.

Children:	Sex	Birth	Death
George Norris	M	10 Apr 1811 Lenham, Kent England	09 Dec 1871 Charing, Kent England
John Norris	M	Abt. 1813 Harrietsham, Kent Eng	Aft. 1871
Thomas Norris	M	Abt. 1818 Lenham, Kent England	
James Norris	M	23 Apr 1820 Lenham, Kent England	
William Norris	M	20 Jan 1822 Lenham, Kent England	
Mary Norris	F	04 Apr 1824 Lenham, Kent England	
Richard Norris	M	02 Apr 1826 Lenham, Kent England	31 Oct 1858 Lenham, Kent England
Jesse Norris	M	Abt. 1829 Lenham, Kent England	Aft. Dec 1871

Children:	Sex	Birth	Death
Sarah Norris	F	Abt. 1831 Lenham, Kent England	30 Jun 1837 Lenham, Kent England
Edward Norris	M	27 Sep 1832 Lenham, Kent England	30 Nov 1855 Lenham, Kent England

We find newspaper accounts of Thomas winning prizes in 1838, 1848 and 1854 for his ploughing and farm skills.

PLOUGHS.

To the best ploughman, with a turn-rise or other plough with 4 horses (£3)—Thomas Norris, ploughman to Mr. William Howland. The driver (15s.)—Richard Shirley.

To the second best ploughman (£2)—James Brown, ploughman to Mr. Thomas Avery. The driver (10s.)—John Brown, sen.

To the third best ploughman (£1 10s.)—Thomas Swadden, ploughman to Mr. Henry Pye. The driver (7s. 6d.)—David Morgan.

To the fourth best ploughman (£1)—Day Filmer, ploughman to Mr. Wm. Powell. The driver (5s.)—Charles Wood.

There were 13 unsuccessful; the waggoners received 5s. each, and the drivers 2s. 6d. each.

There was no competitors for two-horse ploughs, but £1 was awarded to John Norris, ploughman to Mr. Joseph Bishop.

SHEPHERDS.

Figure 3: South Eastern Gazette - Tuesday 30 October 1838

LENHAM AGRICULTURAL ASSOCIATION.

PRIZES AWARDED 27th OCT., 1848.

PLOUGHS.—£3 to Jas. Filmer and 15s. to Wm. Filmer, ploughman and mate of Mr. Wm. Powell.

£2 to John Tassell and 10s. to George Howard, ploughman and mate of Mr. Jno. Roper.

£1 10s. to Thomas Norris and 7s. 6d. to John Johnson, ploughman and mate of Mr. Clark Maylam.

£1 to Richard Day and 5s. to George Copping, ploughman and mate of Mr. Clark Maylam.

10s. to Wm. White and 2s. 6d. to Wm. Banes, ploughman and mate of Mr. Thos. Weston.

A gratuity of £1 to Jas. Vidion, 2-horse ploughman of Mr. Wm. Powell, there not being sufficient competition.

Figure 4: South Eastern Gazette - Tuesday 31 October 1848

PRIZES FOR STACK BUILDING AND THATCHING.

To the best stack builder.............................. 1 0 0

Awarded to Abraham Miles, servant to Mr. W. Powell, Lenham.

To the second best, ditto.............................. 0 10 0

Awarded to Thomas Norris, servant to Mr. Maylam, Lenham.

Figure 5: Maidstone Journal and Kentish Advertiser - Tuesday 28 November 1854 (Denham Agricultural Association)

1841 census Lenham, p 15
Chapman Cottage
NORRIS, Thomas, 50, Ag. Lab
Mary, 50
James, 20
Richard, 14
Jesse 12

Sarah 10
Edward 8
p. 13 is Hannah Golden [sic] and her family

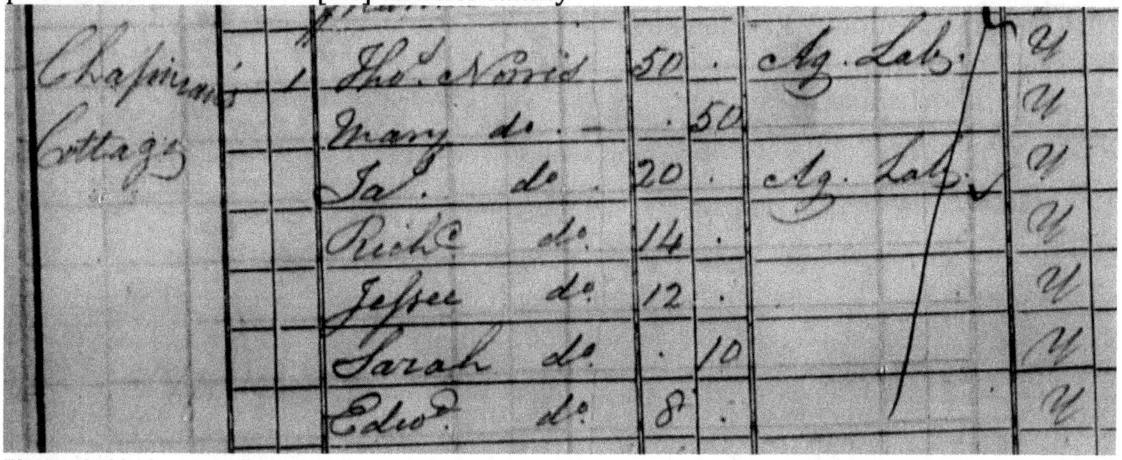

Chapman's Cottage	1	Thos. Norris	50		Ag. Lab.	Y
		Mary do.		50		Y
		Jas. do.	20		Ag. Lab.	Y
		Richd. do.	14			Y
		Jessee do.	12			Y
		Sarah do.		10		Y
		Edwd. do.	8			Y

Figure 6: 1841 census Ramsgate

<u>1851 census Lenham</u>
32 Chapman Cottage
NORRIS, Thomas, 62, Agricultural Labourer, b. Lenham
Mary, 63, b Pluckley
James, 30 b Lenham
Jesse, 22 b Lenham
Sarah, 20 b Lenham
On the next page we see Hannah Golding with her children so it is obvious that Hannah knew Thomas Norris quite well.

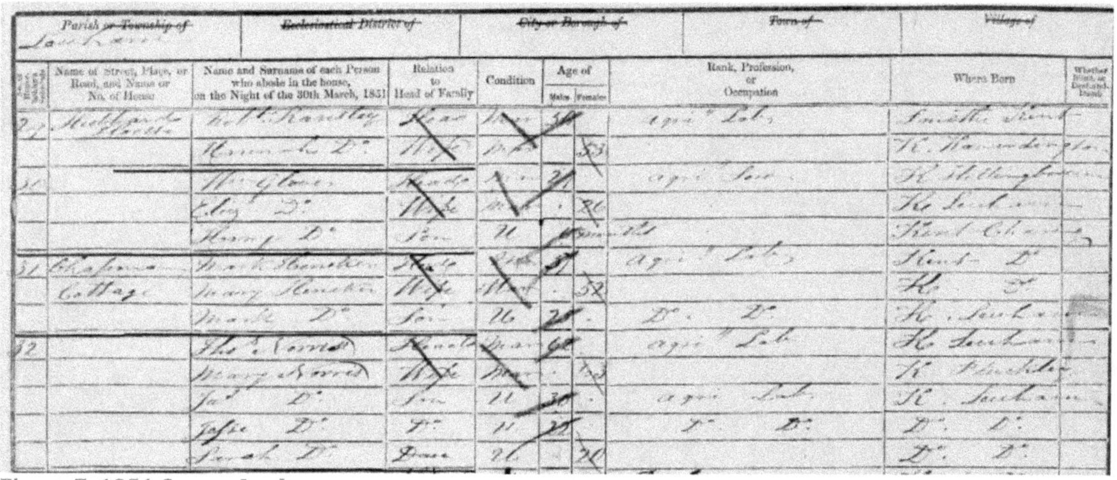

Parish or Township of Lenham | Ecclesiastical District of | City or Borough of | Town of | Village of

No. of Householder's Schedule	Name of Street, Place, or Road, and Name or No. of House	Name and Surname of each Person who abode in the house, on the Night of the 30th March, 1851	Relation to Head of Family	Condition	Age of Males	Age of Females	Rank, Profession, or Occupation	Where Born	Whether Blind, or Deaf-and-Dumb
32		Thos. Norris	Head	Mar	62		Agri. Lab.	K. Lenham	
		Mary Norris	Wife	Mar		63		K. Pluckley	
		Jas. Do.	Son	U	30		Agri. Lab.	K. Lenham	
		Jesse Do.	Do.	U	22		Do. Do.	Do. Do.	
		Sarah Do.	Dau.	U		20		Do. Do.	

Figure 7: 1851 Census Lenham

On 28 January 1859 Thomas was buried in Lenham in St Mary Churchyard. He was noted as being 69 years old.

1861 finds his widow Mary still in Lenham.

1861 census Lenham
p. 82. 14 Chapman Lane
NORRIS, Mary, widow, 74, b Pluckley
George, son, 50, Ag. Lab. b Lenham
John, son, 48 b Lenham
Jesse, son, 32 b Lenham

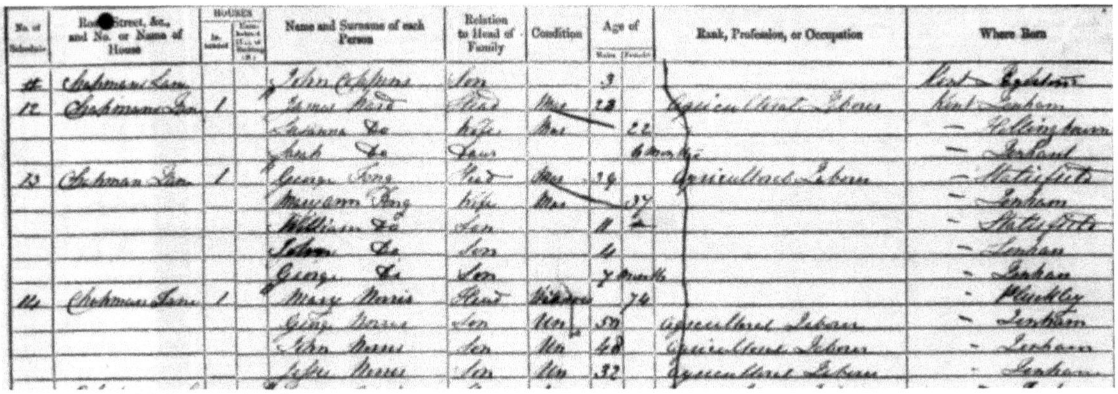

Figure 8: 1861 Census Lenham

This 1861 census is the last record found for Mary. Her son George, 50 and not married, is in this census with her. He my 3rd great-grandfather and the father of my illegitimate 2nd great-grandmother Georgiana Golding baptised in 1840.

Family Group Sheet for Thomas Norris

Husband:		Thomas Norris
	b:	10 May 1789 in Lenham, Kent England
	d:	28 Jan 1859 in Lenham, Kent England
	m:	17 Sep 1809 in All Saints, Maidstone England
	Father:	Edward Norris
	Mother:	Catharine Earl
Wife:		Mary Spicer
	b:	Bet. 1788-1791 in Pluckley, Kent England
	d:	Aft. 1861
	Father:	
	Mother:	

Children:		
1	Name:	George Norris
M	b:	10 Apr 1811 in Lenham, Kent England
	d:	09 Dec 1871 in Charing, Kent England
	Spouse:	Hannah Philpott
2	Name:	John Norris
M	b:	Abt. 1813 in Harrietsham, Kent Eng
	d:	Aft. 1871
3	Name:	Thomas Norris
M	b:	Abt. 1818 in Lenham, Kent England
	m:	25 May 1844 in Lenham, Kent England
	Spouse:	Maria Hopkins
4	Name:	James Norris
M	b:	23 Apr 1820 in Lenham, Kent England
5	Name:	William Norris
M	b:	20 Jan 1822 in Lenham, Kent England
6	Name:	Mary Norris
F	b:	04 Apr 1824 in Lenham, Kent England
7	Name:	Richard Norris
M	b:	02 Apr 1826 in Lenham, Kent England
	d:	31 Oct 1858 in Lenham, Kent England
8	Name:	Jesse Norris
M	b:	Abt. 1829 in Lenham, Kent England
	d:	Aft. Dec 1871
9	Name:	Sarah Norris
F	b:	Abt. 1831 in Lenham, Kent England
	d:	30 Jun 1837 in Lenham, Kent England
10	Name:	Edward Norris
M	b:	27 Sep 1832 in Lenham, Kent England
	d:	30 Nov 1855 in Lenham, Kent England
	m:	18 Oct 1852 in Lenham, Kent England
	Spouse:	Sarah Ann Norris

George Norris 1811-1871 & Hannah Philpot Golding

It has not been easy to learn much about my presumed 3rd great-grandfather George Norris and his life. His baptism took place in Lenham on 10 April 1811 to parents Thomas and Mary.

I have not found him in the 1841 census for Lenham although his parents and siblings were there. It seems that 30 year old George may be living and working elsewhere. Could his disappearance have anything to do with his siring the illegitimate daughter (my 2nd great-grandmother) of the widow Hannah Golding in 1840? George and his family lived next door to Hannah in Lenham and with the naming of her illegitimate daughter Georgiana, and Georgiana naming George Norris as her father when she married Charles Fuller in 1858 we have some pretty compellling evidence to support this George Norris as the father.

1845 finds George winning a ploughing match in Lenham.

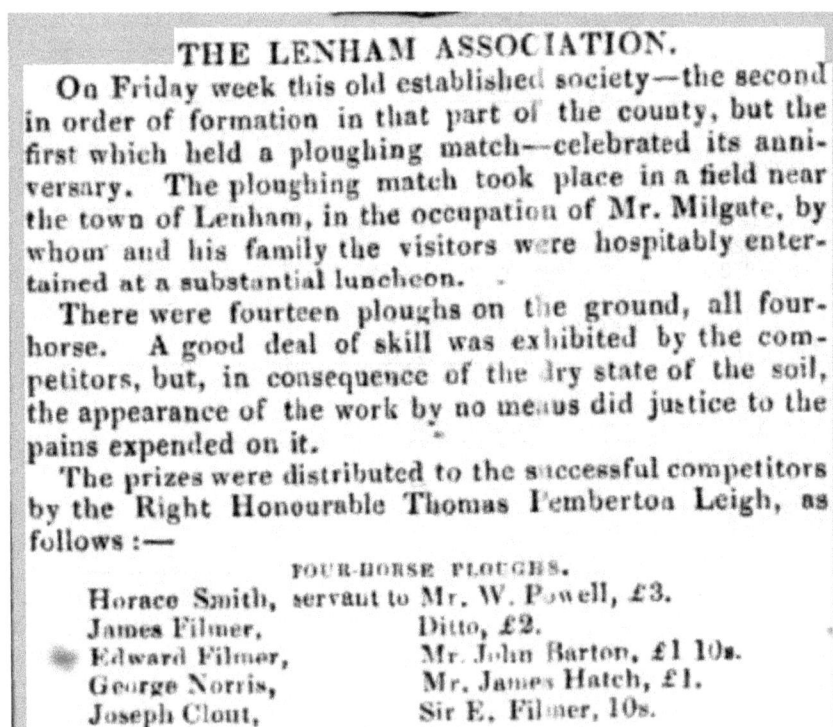

Figure 9: 1845 George Norris wins 4 horse ploughing match

1851 census Lenham, Kent
HO107 piece 1618 folio 225 page 3
Timbold Hill, Lenham
Thomas PHILPOT head age 62 farmer of 104 acres born Ashford
Sarah wife age 77 born Pluckley
George NORRIS single age 36 waggoner born Harrietsham
George CASON age 17 waggoner's mate born Lenham

Jane HEMSLEY age 14 general servant born Bredgar

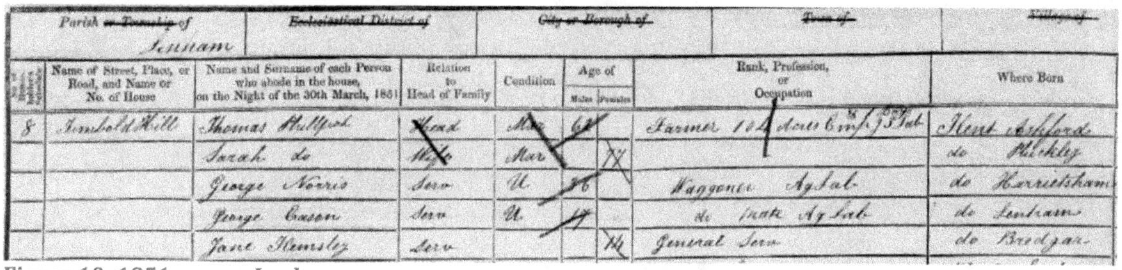

Parish or Township of Lenham		Ecclesiastical District of		City or Borough of			Town of	Village of
No. of Householder's Schedule	Name of Street, Place, or Road, and Name or No. of House	Name and Surname of each Person who abode in the house, on the Night of the 30th March, 1851	Relation to Head of Family	Condition	Age of Males	Age of Females	Rank, Profession, or Occupation	Where Born
8	Tumbold Hill	Thomas Hullock	Head	Mar	68		Farmer 104 acres Emp 3 Lab	Kent Ashford
		Sarah do	Wife	Mar		77		do Pluckley
		George Norris	Serv	U	36		Waggoner Ag Lab	do Harrietsham
		George Eason	Serv	U	17		do (male) Ag Lab	do Lenham
		Jane Hemsley	Serv			14	General Serv	do Bredgar

Figure 10: 1851 census Lenham

<u>1861 census Lenham, 14 Chapman Lane</u>

George Norris, age 50, with mother, unmarried b Lenham, Agricultural Labourer.

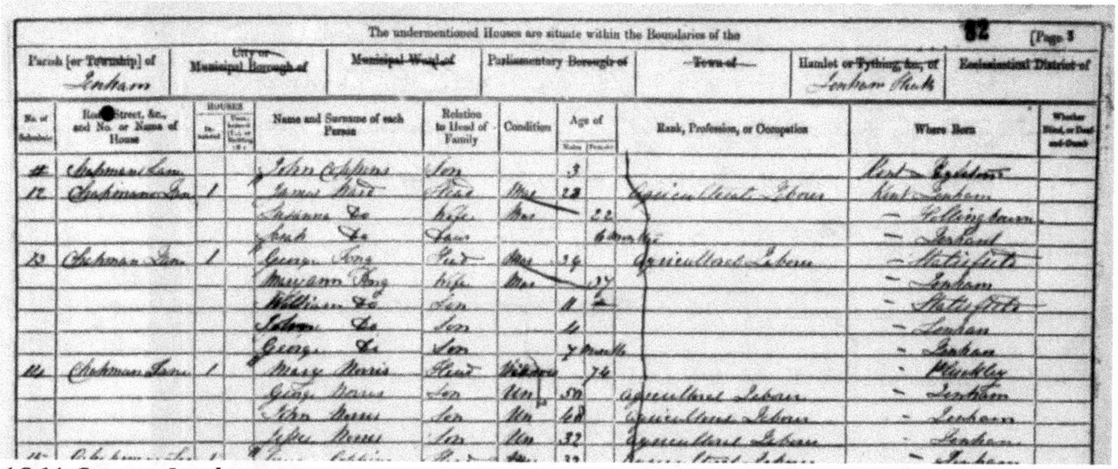

The undermentioned Houses are situate within the Boundaries of the [Page 3] 82

Parish [or Township] of Lenham	City or Municipal Borough of	Municipal Ward of	Parliamentary Borough of	Town of	Hamlet or Tything, &c., of Lenham Street	Ecclesiastical District of				
No. of Schedule	Road, Street, &c., and No. or Name of House	Houses Inhabited	Name and Surname of each Person	Relation to Head of Family	Condition	Age of Males	Age of Females	Rank, Profession, or Occupation	Where Born	Whether Blind, or Deaf-and-Dumb
11	Chapman Lane		John Cobbins	Son		3			Kent Egerton	
12	Chapman Lane	1	James Ward	Head	Mar	23		Agricultural Labourer	Kent Lenham	
			Susanna Do	Wife	Mar		22		Wittersham	
			Ann Do	Daur			6 months		Lenham	
13	Chapman Lane	1	George King	Head	Mar	34		Agricultural Labourer	Stalisfield	
			Maryann King	Wife	Mar		37		Lenham	
			William Do	Son		11			Stalisfield	
			John Do	Son		4			Lenham	
			George Do	Son		7 months			Lenham	
14	Chapman Lane	1	Mary Norris	Head	Widow		74		Pluckley	
			George Norris	Son	Un	50		Agricultural Labourer	Lenham	
			John Norris	Son	Un	48		Agricultural Labourer	Lenham	
			Jesse Norris	Son	Un	37		Agricultural Labourer	Lenham	

1861 Census Lenham

George never married. He died on 9 December 1871 and was buried on December 13th.

His estate was settled in 1872

1872.

NORRIS George.

Effects under £100.

6 January. Administration of the effects of George Norris late of Charing in the County of Kent Labourer a Bachelor who died 9 December 1871 at Charing was granted at Canterbury to Jesse Norris of Lenham in the said County Labourer the Brother and one of the Next of Kin.

Figure 11: England & Wales, National Probate Calendar (Index of Wills and Administrations), 1858-1966, 1973-1995

ON the *Sixth* — day of *January* — 18*72*,
Letters of Administration of all and singular the personal Estate and Effects
of *George Norris late of Charing in the County*
of Kent Labourer — — —

— —

deceased, who died on the *9th* day of *December* 18*71*,
at *Charing aforesaid a Bachelor without Parent*
and intestate — — —

were granted at the District Registry attached to Her Majesty's Court of Probate at
Canterbury — to *Jesse Norris of Lenham*
in the said County of Kent Labourer the
natural and lawful Brother and one of the
next of Kin — — —

— — —

of the said deceased, he having been first sworn duly to administer.

Sureties *Thomas Barten of Lenham in the County of Kent*
Farmer and Edward Barten of Lenham aforesaid
Farmer

Effects under £ *100 No leaseholds*
Extracted by *J. D. Norwood*
Solicitor
Ashford.

N:*exd J.N.P*
Printed for
Her Majesty's Stationery Office,
Princes Street, Storey's Gate,
Westminster.
Cl. Cler:
G (32) 10,000 10/69

Hannah Philpot deserves her own chapter or two. Born in 1802 in Pluckley, which is known as "the most haunted village in England", Hannah must have been aware of the local legends of ghostly apparitions in her village. Her parents John and Susanna Philpot must have come from another parish for they do not appear in the church registers of Pluckley until the baptism of their son James in May 1802. Their marriage has not been found so we do not know Susanna's maiden name.

Three children were found being baptised in the church in Pluckley – James baptised May 1802, Hannah baptised April 1805, and Sarah baptised November 1806. No other children were found.

We know that Hannah's father John Philpot was born around 1774 as his burial record notes that he was 46 years old when he died. His burial was recorded in the parish church on 24 September 1820. His widow Susanna was buried from the same church on 18 June 1837.

Hannah Philpot left Pluckley for Lenham and there she married Edward Golding.

Edward GOLDEN married Hannah PHILPOT 2 March 1823, St. Mary's Lenham. Witnesses: James Philpot & Mary Ralph (their marks). I think the register said "of age" for Edward and "minor" for Hannah

The baptisms of six children born to Edward and Hannah are found in St. Mary's church registers in Lenham – Louisa, James, Sarah, Eliza, Jane and Emily. Less than a year after Emily's birth, Hannah's husband Edward died. His burial took place from St. Mary's Church on 27 June 1837. He was 37 years old.

In July 1840 Hannah's illegitimate daughter Georgiana was born. The 1841 Census for 1841 shows the widow Hannah living in Swan's Cottage on Lenham Heath with her seven children ages 1 to 17.

In March 1843 an illegitimate son Edward John was born to Hannah. Georgiana gave her father's name as George Norris on her marriage record but we do not at this time know who Edward John's father was. Both illegitimate children used the Golding (aka Golden) surname.

1851 shows Hannah is earning money to support herself and her family by working as a charwoman. In 1871 she is recorded as a 68 year old farm labourer. On 1 July 1873 poor Hannah was admitted to the local Insane Asylum in Maidstone where she died on 25 April 1881.

It is interesting but sad to note that Hannah's daughter Georgiana was in the same asylum in 1864 and again in 1868.

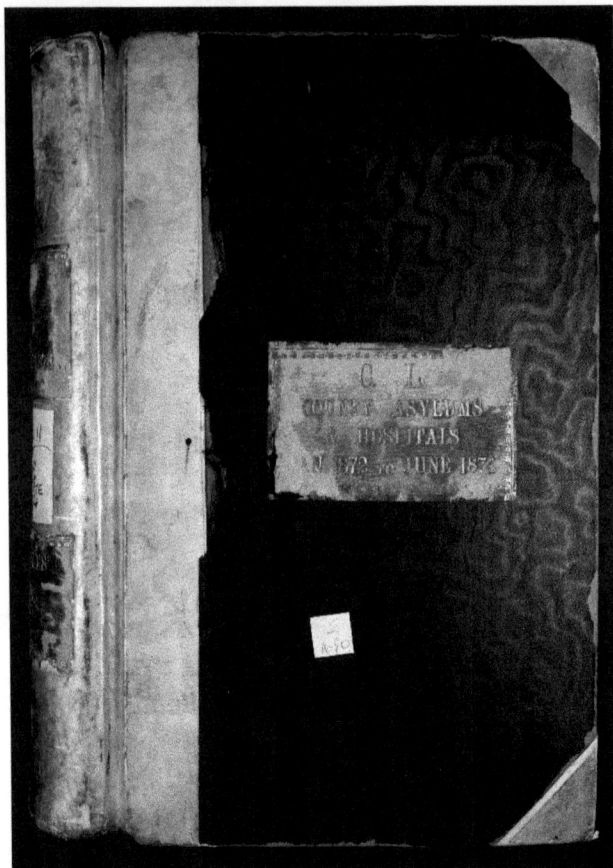

Lunacy Admissions in County Asylums & Hospitals

Bottom line is entry for Hannah Golding

Kent County Lunatic Asylum, now known as Oakwood

Georgiana Golding 1840-1882 & Charles Fuller

My 2nd great-grandmother Georgiana Golding was born in 1840 in Lenham Kent. She was the illegitimate daughter of Hannah Golding, widow - daughter Georgiana baptised 12 July 1840

On her marriage certificate, Georgiana gave her father's name as George Norris

Marriage in St. Mary's Parish Church, Lenham. Entry #221:

Oct 17, 1858: Charles Fuller, of age, bachelor, labourer Lenham. Father: John Fuller, labourer. Charles married Georgiana Golding, minor, spinster Lenham. Father of Georgiana given as George Norris, labourer. Married in the Parish church after banns. Witnesses: George & Sarah Earl. Neither groom, bride nor witnesses were literate, all signing with their marks. Marriage Certificate, Parish of Lenham, Hollingbourne District, Kent.

After their marriage Georgiana began having children quite regularly – Frederick 1859, Elizabeth 1861, and Harriet in 1864. Just three months after Harriet's birth Georgiana was committed to the Insane Asylum in Kent. Admitted April 22, 1864 she was discharged 4 months later on 1 September that same year. Did she suffer from post-partum depression? Her husband was responsible for three children ages 4 months, 3 years and 5 years for those months while she was in the asylum and I wonder who helped look after them.

22 April 1864 Georgiana Fuller admitted to Kent Insane Asylum. Discharged on 1 September 1864

A few months after her discharge Georgiana was pregnant again and in September 1865 she gave birth to her fourth child, Martha. Next came Charles, my great-grandfather, born 1867, followed by Alfred born October 1868. But in April 1868 when young Charles was 7 months old and Georgiana was 3 months pregnant with Alfred, she was once again committed to the Insane Asylum. Perhaps it was post-partum depression or simply the fact that she had five children under the age of 11 and one more on the way. In any case she was in the Asylum for five months then discharged.

No. Order of Admission.	Name.	Private. M.	Private. F.	Pauper. M.	Pauper. F.	Date of Admission. 1868	Asylum,	Date of Discharge or Death.	Discharged. Recovd.	Discharged. Relievd.	Discharged. Not Impvd.	Died.
26,095	Fletcher Eleanor		1			20 Mar	Bethlem	15 Feb 69				
26,096	Forster William				1	28 Mar	Morpeth	1 Ap 72				1
26,139	Franzoni Bartolomeo	1				28 Mar	Bethlem	18 Dec 68		1		
26,140	Fletcher Robt			1		30 Mar	Chester	3 Dec 68				
26,141	Flint Ann				1	31 Mar	Derby	2 Feb 74				1
26,178	Foxton Mary				1	12 Ap	Lincoln	27 Jan 70	1			
26,225	Futrell Jno.			1		1 Ap	Stafford	27 June 71	1			
26,226	Fathers Chas			1		17 Ap	North'ton	11 July 68	1			
26,290	Fathers Ann				1	3 Ap	Dorset	7 Oct 70	1			
26,343	Ford Mary S.		1			6 Ap	St Lukes	6 June 68				
26,344	Folkes Mary				1	7 Ap	Lincoln	22 June 68				1
26,456	Featherstone Rebeka				1	8 Ap	Notts	2 May 68				1
26,518	Foote William C.			1		13 Ap	Colney H.	4 Dec 68				1
26,556	Freeman Geo.			1		13 Ap	Suffolk	11 Ap 74		1		
26,557	Fleetwood Joseph			1		13 Ap	Worcester	26 Jan 82			1	1
26,558	Flynn Margt				1	17 Ap	Denbigh	22 Dec 68	1			
26,585	Fisher Susannah				1	16 Ap	Birmingham	31 Dec 75				1
26,620	Flower Mary				1	20 Ap	N. York	9 Dec 90				1
26,635	Firth Sarah				1	21 Ap	"	20 Nov 68	1			
26,644	Fairbrother Elizth				1	22 Ap	Lancaster	3 June 74				1
26,665	Fletcher Thos.			1		23 Ap	Salop	18 Nov 68				
26,666	Franklyn Mark			1		23 Ap	Wilts	11 May 68				1
26,700	Fuller Georgiana				1	21 Ap	Kent	18 Sep 68	1			
26,701	Ferriday Mary				1	23 Ap	Salop	15 July 68				

21 Apr 1868 Georgiana Fuller admitted to Kent Lunatic Asylum. Discharged 18 September 1868

Georgiana had five more children born after Alfred in 1868 – Mene 1871, Edward/Edwin 1874, Walter 1877 and Albert 1879. In 1882 when pregnant with her 11th child she died.

Georgiana died in childbirth in October 1882. She was 44 years old.

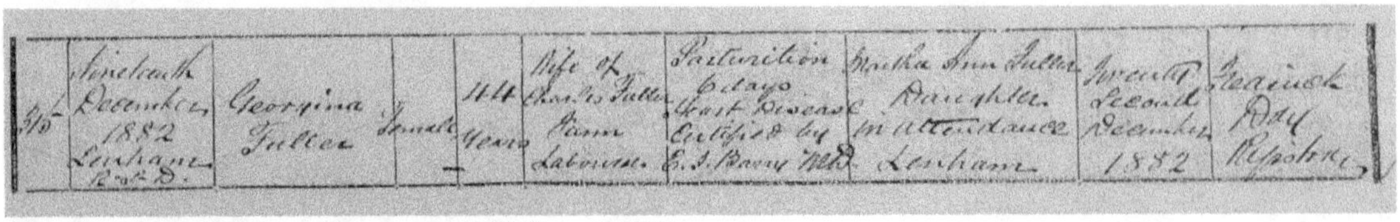

315	Nineteenth December 1882 Lenham R.S.D.	Georgina Fuller	Female	44 Years	Wife of Charles Fuller Farm Labourer	Parturition 6 days Heart Disease Certified by E. J. Barry MD	Martha Ann Fuller Daughter In attendance Lenham	Twenty second December 1882	Frederick Day Registrar

Death Certificate Georgiana Golding 1882

Norris Ancestors of Elmsted and Waltham Kent

This Norris line daughtered out with the birth of my 6th great-grandmother Sarah Norris in Waltham in 1743. Sarah married Francis Allard in 1769 but we can trace her Norris ancestors back to my 9th great-grandfather John Norris born circa 1655.

We know nothing of John Norris other than the birth of a son in Elmsted. John Norris Jr. was baptised 08 February 1680 but his mother's name was not recorded.

It is not, at this point, known whether these two Norris lines are related. Perhaps a descendant will be intrigued enough to do further research.

St. James the Great, Elmsted Kent

St. Bartholomew Church in Waltham Kent

Image copyright owned by John Salmon and licensed for reuse under the Creative Commons Attribution-ShareAlike 2.0 license.

John Norris 1690-1740 & Mary Carr

On 8 February 1680 the baptism of my 8th great-grandfather John Norris took place in St James the Great in Elmstead Kent.

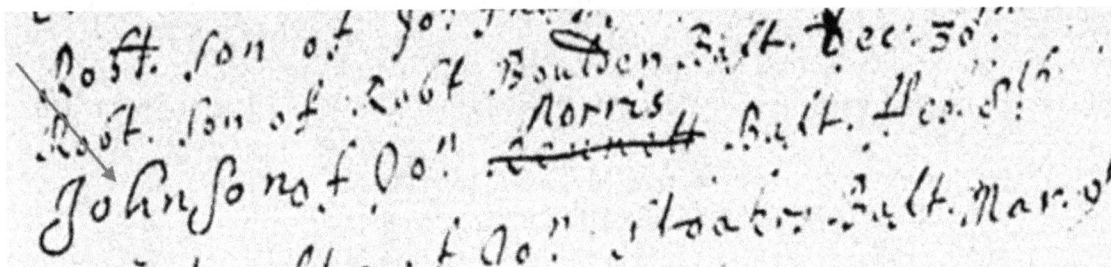

John son of John Norris bapt. Feb. 8th

John married Mary Carr in Waltham in 1710. She may have been the Mary Carr baptised on 08 Mar 1684 in Chartham, St Mary to Edward and Catherine Carr. She did name a son Edward and a daughter Catherine so this is a good fit for her parents but more research is needed for absolute proof.

Chartham is a small village about 7 miles from Waltham. Waltham has been associated in the past with the Knights Templar and was originally called Temple Waltham, with a Chantry next to St Bartholomew. Elmstead is only 9 miles from Chartham.

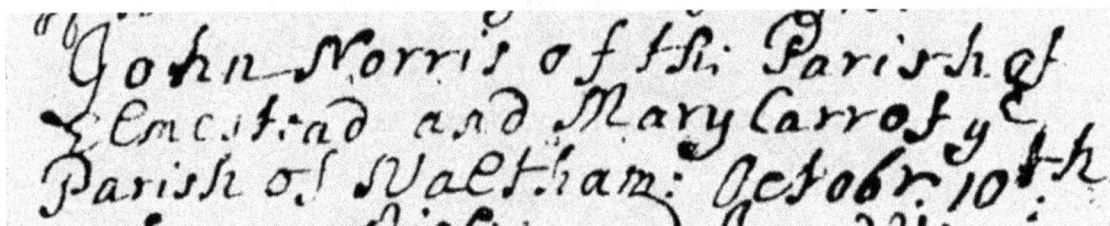

John Norris of this Parish of Elmestead (sic) and Mary Carr of ye Parish of Waltham. October 10th.

Baptisms of eight children born to John and Mary (Carr) Norris have been found in the church registers of St. Bartholomew in Waltham. St. Bartholomew was built in the 13th century and has a vantage point above the Duckpitt Valley.

Family Group Sheet for John Norris

Husband:		John Norris
	b:	08 Feb 1680 in Elmsted, St James the Great, Kent, England
	d:	28 Feb 1740 in Elmsted, Kent, England; buried in woolen
	m:	10 Oct 1710 in Waltham, Kent, England
	Father:	John Norris
	Mother:	
Wife:		Mary Carr
	b:	Bet. 1680-1685 in Waltham Kent England
	Father:	
	Mother:	

Children:		
1	Name:	Mary Norris
F	b:	25 Mar 1711 in Waltham St. Bartholomew, Kent
2	Name:	John Norris
M	b:	13 Jan 1712 in Waltham St. Bartholomew, Kent
3	Name:	Thomas Norris
M	b:	20 Feb 1714 in Waltham St. Bartholomew, Kent
	m:	30 Dec 1739 in Canterbury St. Mildred, Kent
	Spouse:	Sarah Boughton
4	Name:	William Norris
M	b:	22 Feb 1716 in Waltham St. Bartholomew, Kent
5	Name:	Elizabeth Norris
F	b:	05 Nov 1721 in Waltham St. Bartholomew, Kent
6	Name:	Stephen Norris
M	b:	13 Dec 1725 in Waltham St. Bartholomew, Kent
7	Name:	Catherine Norris
F	b:	04 Jun 1727 in Waltham St. Bartholomew, Kent
8	Name:	Edward Norris
M	b:	22 Mar 1729 in Waltham St. Bartholomew, Kent

Thomas Norris 1714-? & Sarah Boughton

Thomas was baptised in St. Bartholomew in Waltham on 20 February 1714 to John Norris and Mary Carr. On 30 December 1739 he married Sarah Boughton at St. Mildred in Canterbury. Sarah was noted as being from the Parish of **St George.**

St. Mildred's Church, Canterbury

Image copyright Robert Cutts from Bristol, England, UK licensed under the Creative Commons Attribution 2.0 Generic license

Family Group Sheet for Thomas Norris

Husband:		Thomas Norris
	b:	20 Feb 1714 in Waltham St. Bartholomew, Kent
	m:	30 Dec 1739 in Canterbury St. Mildred, Kent
	Father:	John Norris
	Mother:	Mary Carr
Wife:		Sarah Boughton
	b:	St. George, Canterbury England
	Father:	
	Mother:	
Children:		
1	Name:	William Norris
M	b:	Bet. 1739-1745
	d:	14 Nov 1745 in Waltham, St. Bartholomew, Kent England
2	Name:	Thomas Norris
M	b:	19 Apr 1741 in Waltham, St Bartholomew
3	Name:	Sarah Norris
F	b:	31 Jul 1743 in Waltham Kent England
	m:	19 Dec 1769 in Wye, Ss Gregory & Martin, Kent
	Spouse:	Francis Alllard
4	Name:	Susannah Norris
F	b:	26 Apr 1745 in Waltham, St Bartholomew
5	Name:	William Norris
M	b:	31 Aug 1746 in Waltham, St Bartholomew
6	Name:	Lydia Norris
F	b:	11 Sep 1748 in Waltham, St Bartholomew
	d:	30 Oct 1748 in Waltham, St. Bartholomew, Kent England

Sarah Norris 1743-1821 & Francis Allard

6th great-grandmother Sarah Norris was baptised on 31 July 1743 in Waltham Kent England.

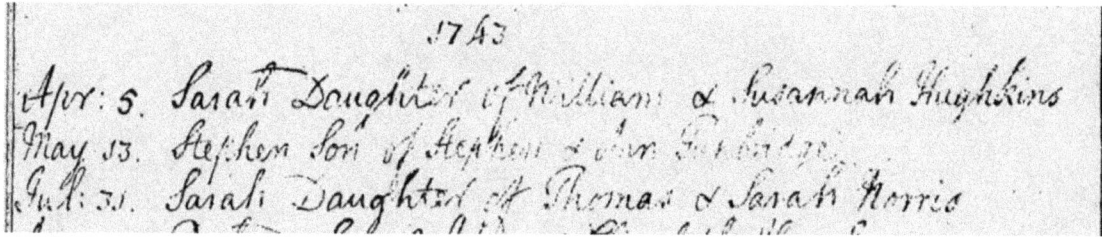

1743 Baptism in Waltham

At the age of 26 she married Francis Allard on 19 December 1769 in Wye, Saints Gregory & Martin. Francis was baptised in Wye on 06 January 1744 to parents James Allard and Elizabeth Brown.

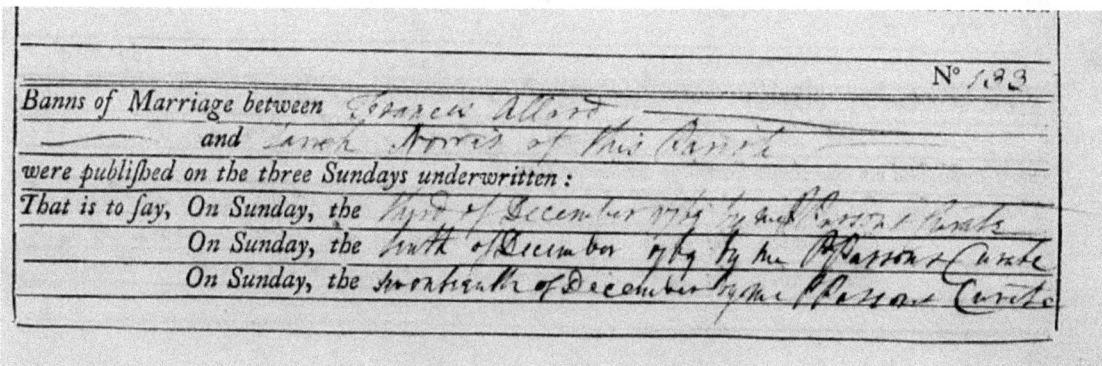

Banns for Francis Allard and Sarah Norris December 1769

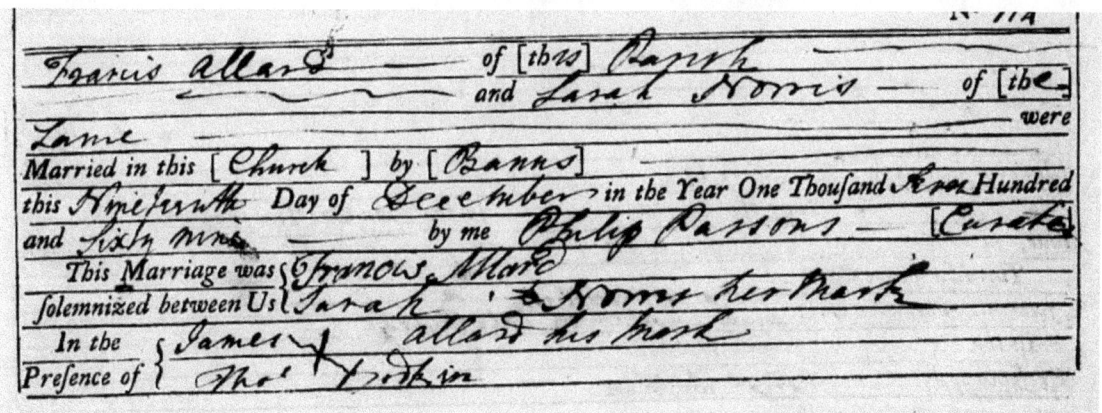

Marriage of Francis Allard and Sarah Norris 19 December 1769

1744 Baptism of Francis Allard son of James Allard and Mary Drury

Notes

www.ingramcontent.com/pod-product-compliance
Lightning Source LLC
Chambersburg PA
CBHW051349290326
41933CB00042B/3345